DRAGSTERS

by
Sean McCollum

Consultant:

Jeff Burk, Editor/Publisher
DragRacingOnline.com

CAPSTONE PRESS
a capstone imprint

Edge Books are published by Capstone Press,
151 Good Counsel Drive, P.O. Box 669, Mankato, Minnesota 56002.
www.capstonepress.com

Printed in the United States of America in Stevens Point, Wisconsin.
092009
005619WZS10

 Books published by Capstone Press are manufactured with paper
containing at least 10 percent post-consumer waste.

Library of Congress Cataloging-in-Publication Data
McCollum, Sean.
Dragsters / by Sean McCollum.
    p. cm. — (Edge Books. Full throttle)
    Summary: "Describes the history, features, and performance of dragsters" — Provided
by publisher.
    Includes bibliographical references and index.
    ISBN 978-1-4296-3941-5 (library binding)
    1. Dragsters — Juvenile literature. 2. Drag racing — Juvenile literature. I. Title.
TL236.2.M33 2010
796.72 — dc22   2009028652

Editorial Credits
Abby Czeskleba, editor; Tracy Davies, designer; Jo Miller, media researcher;
    Laura Manthe, production specialist

Photo Credits
Auto Imagery, Inc., 5, 7, 8, 9, 12, 13, 15, 17, 18, 21, 22, 23, 25, 27 (both), 28,
    29 (top), cover
CORBIS/Icon SMI/David Allio, 29 (bottom)
Getty Images Inc./Alvis Upitis, 11 (bottom)
Getty Images Inc./WireImage/Bob Riha Jr, 11 (top)

Artistic Effects
Dreamstime/In-finity; Dreamstime/Michaelkovachev; iStockphoto/Michael Irwin;
iStockphoto/Russell Tate; Shutterstock/Els Jooren; Shutterstock/Fedorov Oleksiy;
Shutterstock/jgl247; Shutterstock/Marilyn Volan; Shutterstock/Pocike

Table of Contents

SPEED TO BURN

John Force revved the engine of his green and white Mustang funny car. His challenger rolled up to the starting line in the next lane. The race was for first place at the 2008 Southern Nationals at Atlanta Dragway. The lights flashed yellow, then green. The cars launched down the track, turning tire rubber into smoke.

In the blink of an eye, the sprint down the ¼-mile (.4-kilometer) track was over. Ashley Force had beaten her dad fair and square. She completed her **pass** in less than five seconds, clocking a speed of more than 320 miles (515 kilometers) per hour.

pass — a dragster's run down the drag strip

Ashley Force (white car) raced her father (green car) at the 2008 Southern Nationals.

Fast Fact: The pole of lights that signals the start of a drag race is called the Christmas tree.

ULTIMATE SPEEDSTERS

Dragsters are the ultimate speedsters of the motorsports world. Their sleek shapes and large engines help the cars **accelerate** quickly. They don't race around oval courses. Instead, most drag races take place on $1/8$-mile (.2-kilometer) or $1/4$-mile (.4-kilometer) strips.

More than 200 classes of vehicles race on drag strips in the United States. The vehicles include motorcycles, pickup trucks, and street roadsters. Some dragster classes are organized by the type of fuel the vehicles use.

Three classes of dragsters get the most attention in pro drag racing today. These headliners are the top fuelers, pro stock cars, and funny cars.

TOP FUELERS

Top fuelers are long, narrow dragsters. They get their name from nitromethane, the fuel they use. Their wide racing **slicks** grab the track. A large rear wing and two small front wings help the driver control the car. The powerful engine is mounted behind the driver's seat. Most teams use an aluminum model of the Chrysler Hemi engine. Top fuelers reach speeds of more than 330 miles (531 kilometers) per hour.

Front and back wings push down on a top fueler to keep it on the track.

accelerate – to gain speed

slick – a racing tire made with a smooth, soft suface to get maximum grip on the track

PRO STOCK

Pro stock cars look a lot like factory-made cars. They are sometimes called factory hot rods. But they are built for drag racing, inside and out. Their engines crank out more than 1,300 **horsepower**. That power accelerates the car to more than 200 miles (322 kilometers) per hour in less than seven seconds.

Pro stock cars look similar to highway vehicles.

horsepower — a unit for measuring an engine's power

FUNNY CARS

Funny cars are like a mix of top fuelers and pro stock cars. The outer body looks like a pro stock car. But funny cars use the same fuel and engine as top fuelers. Unlike top fuelers, the engine is set in the front of the car.

Funny cars are front-engine vehicles.

Drag racing got its start among young California car buffs in the 1930s. Friends teamed up to rebuild and tune-up old cars for fun. To reduce the car's weight, they cut away fenders and got rid of body panels. They dropped in bigger engines. These "hot rods" were not always beautiful, but they boasted power and speed.

But hot rods also had a dangerous downside. To see who had the fastest car, drivers challenged each other to race on public roads. These street races were against the law and led to deadly wrecks.

A few hot rod fans came up with a way to safely control this need for speed. Wally Parks loved fast cars, but he wanted illegal racing off the streets. He helped organize timed hot rod races at places like old airfields. These events stressed safety and fun. In 1951, Parks became editor of *Hot Rod* magazine. That same year, he helped form the National Hot Rod Association (NHRA). The NHRA held its first official race in 1953. The organization developed rules and standards to make drag racing a real sport.

Wally Parks celebrated the NHRA's 50th year in 2001.

Two drivers compete in an NHRA race in 1968.

Fast Fact: The NHRA is the world's largest auto racing organization.

THE FIRST DECADES

In 1955, Dick Craft raced his Mercury V-8 to 110 miles (177 kilometers) per hour for the ¼-mile (.4-kilometer). Two years later, Emery Cook broke Craft's record when he reached 170 miles (274 kilometers) per hour. Nitromethane helped Cook make his record pass. This fuel releases more energy than regular racing gasoline.

During the 1960s, the NHRA divided dragsters into different groups to make competitions fair. Nitromethane-powered top fuel dragsters were introduced as a professional class in 1963. They were long and narrow. Their engines were set in front of the driver.

Front-engine dragsters became popular in the 1960s.

sponsor — a company or organization that gives a racer equipment or money to race

In 1966, "Dyno Don" Nicholson introduced the flip-top funny car to drag racing. It had a tube frame under the body of a 1966 Comet. Its wheels were set farther forward than other dragsters. This design gave the car better acceleration. Its strange appearance also earned the car its name.

In 1970, pro stock was introduced as a professional class. Professional drag racing had become big business by this time. **Sponsors** poured money into the sport to gain attention. Fun nicknames and rivalries gave the races extra excitement. A fan favorite was the competition between funny car drivers Don "The Snake" Prudhomme and Tom "The Mongoose" McEwen. Prudhomme and McEwen were friends, but they did not let that get in the way of great racing.

Rivals Don "The Snake" Prudhomme and Tom "The Mongoose" McEwen always promised fans exciting races.

DISASTER BRINGS NEW IDEAS

By 1970, "Big Daddy" Don Garlits had become a star of top fuel drag racing. But he had a terrible accident that year while driving his famous front-engine "Swamp Rat." When he started a pass, the transmission exploded. The explosion tore the dragster in two. It also took off part of his right foot.

The next year Garlits was back with a new car that set the drag racing world buzzing. It was a top fueler, but the engine was in the back. The design helped protect the driver in case of an engine problem. Garlits started winning races and championships again. He perfected the rear-engine design. Other dragster teams quickly copied his design.

Another big change appeared in 1984. Joe Amato changed the rear wing mounted on his top fueler. The new wing was placed higher and farther back than other designs. Air rushing over this wing pushed down on the rear of the car, giving it better traction. The look of top fuelers has changed little since then.

Today, the NHRA recognizes more than 200 classes of dragsters. It holds more than 20 national competitions a year. Professional drag racers get most of the attention and money. But amateur racers and their machines also spend time on drag strips. The organization holds races at more than 100 North American tracks. It also sets the competition and safety rules for dragsters.

Don Garlits drove the Swamp Rat 22
at the 1976 NHRA World Finals.

Fast Fact: Don Garlits won
144 national drag racing events
during his career.

TODAY'S DRAGSTERS

Drivers from the early days of drag racing would marvel at today's high-tech dragsters. Whatever the class, dragsters are made for quick acceleration and speed.

PRO STOCK

Like stock cars that race on oval tracks, pro stock dragsters look like regular road cars. Pro stock cars must weigh at least 2,350 pounds (1,066 kilograms). Pro stock car engines can produce more than 1,300 horsepower. These dragsters reach more than 200 miles (322 kilometers) per hour in less than seven seconds.

Rules require that the same company build the pro stock car's engine and chassis. Common pro stock engines include the GM big-block wedge, the Chrysler Hemi, and the Ford wedge. Pro stock engines burn racing gasoline.

A pro stock car's chassis includes the frame and mechanical parts. About 400 feet (122 meters) of chromoly tubing forms the car's skeleton, including the driver's **roll cage**.

A lightweight outer shell covers the chassis. The headlights, taillights, and other features of the body must match factory models like the Chevy Cobalt and Pontiac GTO.

The big hood scoop on pro stock cars gives them their fierce look. This scoop rams air into the car's engine. The air burns with fuel to power the car.

Pro stock cars are known for their large hood scoops.

roll cage — a structure of strong metal tubing in a car that surrounds and protects the driver

Safety in the Fast Lane

Dragsters continue to reach record speeds, but they are also safer than ever. Rear-mounted wheelie bars prevent the cars from flipping backward. Parachutes slow down the cars quickly after a pass. Super-strong roll cages keep drivers from being crushed during a wreck. Funny cars have automatic fire-extinguisher systems to put out fires.

Drivers wear helmets as well as fire-resistant underwear, suits, gloves, and shoes. Cockpits are also outfitted with heavy-duty restraint systems to protect a driver's head and neck.

A top fuel dragster uses parachutes to slow down after a race.

No car better represents drag racing than top fuel dragsters. Drag racing fans sometimes refer to top fuelers as "kings of the sport." These long, lean cars scream speed.

From the front of the car to the back wing, top fuel dragsters are about 25 feet (8 meters) long. The wing does not lift up the car like a wing lifts up an airplane. The dragster's wing creates **downforce** when air rushes over it. Downforce gives top fuelers better traction and more control. Smaller wings mounted on the nose push down on the front of the car.

In top fuelers, the driver sits in front of the engine. Like funny cars, top fuelers use a version of the 426 Chrysler Hemi engine with a **supercharger**. The two classes also use a similar drivetrain and clutch system that automatically shifts gears during a pass. This system transfers power from the engine to the rear wheels.

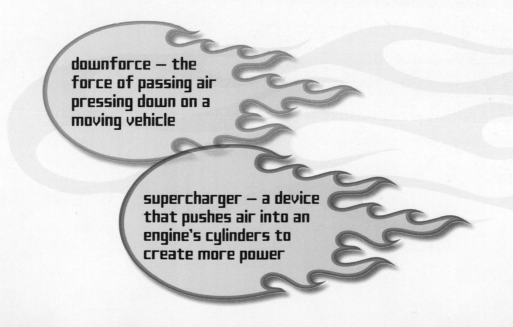

downforce — the force of passing air pressing down on a moving vehicle

supercharger — a device that pushes air into an engine's cylinders to create more power

Funny cars look like pro stock cars on the outside. But their engine and other features perform like top fuelers. Funny cars burn nitromethane fuel and go nearly as fast as top fuelers.

Funny car bodies are lightweight but strong. Molded of super-tough carbon fiber, these shells weigh only about 88 pounds (40 kilograms). Underneath the shell is a frame, which is built of about 180 feet (55 meters) of chromoly tubing. The one-piece shell can be flipped up, giving mechanics quick access to a funny car's engine.

Most funny car teams use the 426 Chrysler Hemi engine. A supercharger is mounted on the engine's air intake to add more horsepower. Superchargers can crank up an engine's power by 50 to 100 percent.

The drivetrain is the system that transfers engine power to a funny car's wheels. Funny car drivetrains use a timer-controlled clutch system. This system handles the high-speed gear shifts, allowing smoother acceleration.

For safety, funny cars must have an escape hatch in the roof. Six-inch (15-centimeter) holes are also built into the side windows. These openings allow fire crews to quickly insert a fire hose.

Mechanics flip up a funny car's shell to work on the engine.

Fast Fact: Racing slicks are under-inflated to help the tires grip the track.

High-speed races make for an exciting day at the drag strip. But understanding the rules makes watching drag racing even more entertaining.

Two pro stock cars race at Thunder Valley Nationals in 2009.

GET READY TO RACE

Cars and drivers perform qualifying runs during the first part of drag racing tournaments. These runs prove which cars are fast enough to race in the main event.

Before each pass, dragster drivers do short burnouts. Water is applied to the big rear slicks. Then the drivers brake hard and spin the rear racing slicks until they smoke. The burnout heats up the slicks and improves the car's traction.

A funny car does a burnout at the 2009 Summit Nationals.

After the burnout, the dragsters roll forward to the starting line. The lights on the Christmas tree tell the drivers where to stop. This part of the race is called staging. Now the drivers focus on the starting lights of the Christmas tree. The drivers hit the throttle as the lights flash green. If a driver leaves too early, the red light flashes and the car fouls out of the race.

When the pass begins, a driver tries to stay in the middle of the lane. Dragsters get better traction in the center of the lane because there is rubber from past burnouts. Drivers must stay in their lanes. Otherwise, the driver is out of the tournament.

One by one, dragsters are **eliminated**. A tournament usually consists of three or four rounds. The winning dragster of each pass moves on to the next race. The winner of the final round takes home the championship.

eliminated – to be removed from a competition by a defeat

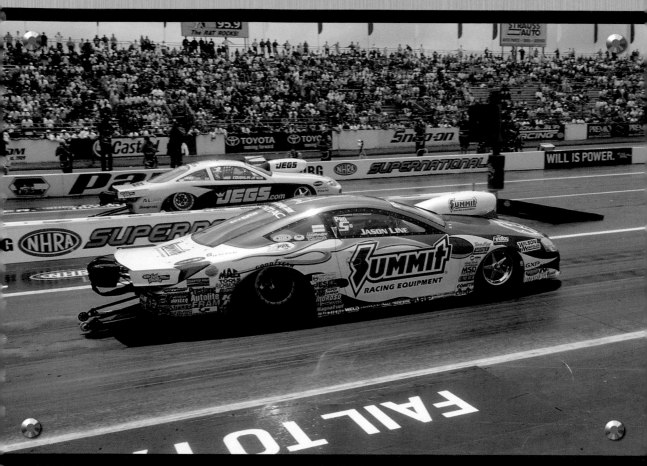

Two pro stock dragsters line up in front of the Christmas tree.

Fast Fact: The center of a lane is called the groove.

MORE THAN SPEED

The most popular form of drag racing is elapsed time (ET) bracket racing. This type of racing allows two cars from different classes to have an equal chance at winning. The racing teams need to be smart, fast, and lucky.

Before a race, the drivers do time trials on the track. Based on these times, the teams guess what their time will be. The time they guess is called the dial-in.

If one car gives its dial-in as 10 seconds, another car may guess a dial-in of nine seconds. The first car gets a one-second head start because the second car had a faster dial-in.

The racing team cannot give a high dial-in to get a head start. During a breakout, a car races faster than its dial-in time. A breakout usually means an automatic loss, even if the car crosses the finish line first.

Quick reflexes often determine who wins the race. Driver reaction time can be used to break a tie. Race officials check each driver's reaction time if the two cars cross the finish line at the same time. The driver with the quicker reaction time wins the race.

A dragster competes in bracket racing at the 2008 Fall Classic National Open.

Bracket racing allows different types of dragsters to have an equal chance at winning.

Like other motorsports, drag racing has a season-long series. Drivers compete for wins and points in order to capture the overall championship. The NHRA Full Throttle Drag Racing Series is the biggest series.

Drag racing brings experienced drivers and new talent together. Tony Schumacher has more than 50 wins under his belt in top fuel dragsters. Antron Brown is a newer star, with big wins in both top fuelers and pro stock motorcycles. Among pro stock cars, Greg Anderson, Jeg Coughlin Jr., and Jason Line often duke it out for the top spots.

In 2008, funny car driver John Force made it into the Motorsports Hall of Fame of America. Force has had more than 125 national wins. His daughter Ashley also races funny cars. Ashley's sisters, Brittany and Courtney, compete in top alcohol dragsters.

Drag racing promises great competition and high-speed thrills. Watching these speedy cars makes for an exciting day at the races.

Tony Schumacher climbs into his top fuel dragster.

Antron Brown has made a name for himself in the drag racing world.

Funny car legend John Force won his 13th NHRA Powerade Championship in 2004.

GLOSSARY

accelerate (ak-SEH-luh-rayt) — to gain speed

burnout (BURN-owt) — when the driver spins the tires before a drag race to get better traction

chassis (CHA-see) — the main framework of a vehicle to which the other parts are fixed

chromoly (KROH-muh-lee) — a mixture of the two metals chromium and molybdenum

downforce (DOUN-fors) — the force of passing air pressing down on a moving vehicle

eliminated (i-LIM-uh-nay-tuhd) — to be removed from a competition by a defeat

horsepower (HORSS-pou-ur) — a unit for measuring an engine's power

pass (PASS) — a dragster's run down the drag strip

roll cage (ROHL KAYJ) — a structure of strong metal tubing in a car that surrounds and protects the driver

slick (SLIK) — a racing tire made with a smooth, soft surface to get maximum grip on the track

sponsor (SPON-sur) — a company or organization that gives a racer equipment or money to race

supercharger (soo-pur-CHARJ-ur) — a device that pushes air into an engine's cylinders to create more power

throttle (THROT-uhl) — a pedal that controls how much fuel and air flow into an engine

traction (TRAK-shuhn) — the grip of a car's tires on the ground

Read More

Gigliotti, Jim. *Hottest Dragsters and Funny Cars.* Wild Wheels! Berkeley Heights, N.J.: Enslow, 2008.

McCollum, Sean. *Racecars: The Ins and Outs of Stock Cars, Dragsters, and Open Wheelers.* RPM. Mankato, Minn.: Capstone Press, 2010.

Zuehlke, Jeffrey. *Drag Racers.* Motor Mania. Minneapolis: Lerner, 2008.

Internet Sites

FactHound offers a safe, fun way to find Internet sites related to this book. All of the sites on FactHound have been researched by our staff.

Here's all you do:

Visit *www.facthound.com*

FactHound will fetch the best sites for you!

Index